WOMEN WHO NEED DONUTS

Honoring Our Cravings ... and Building
a Business and a Life out of Love.

LEIGH KELLIS

BALBOA.
PRESS
A DIVISION OF HAY HOUSE

Balboa Press books may be ordered through booksellers or by contacting:

Balboa Press
A Division of Hay House
1663 Liberty Drive
Bloomington, IN 47403
www.balboapress.com
1 (877) 407-4847

Because of the dynamic nature of the Internet, any web addresses or links contained in this book may have changed since publication and may no longer be valid. The views expressed in this work are solely those of the author and do not necessarily reflect the views of the publisher, and the publisher hereby disclaims any responsibility for them.

The author of this book does not dispense medical advice or prescribe the use of any technique as a form of treatment for physical, emotional, or medical problems without the advice of a physician, either directly or indirectly. The intent of the author is only to offer information of a general nature to help you in your quest for emotional and spiritual well-being. In the event you use any of the information in this book for yourself, which is your constitutional right, the author and the publisher assume no responsibility for your actions.

Any people depicted in stock imagery provided by Getty Images are models, and such images are being used for illustrative purposes only.

Certain stock imagery © Getty Images.

Print information available on the last page.

ISBN: 978-1-5043-9786-5 (sc)
ISBN: 978-1-5043-9788-9 (hc)
ISBN: 978-1-5043-9787-2 (e)

Library of Congress Control Number: 2018901959

Balboa Press rev. date: 03/21/2018

Contents

Contents

Preface

I am the founder of a business in Portland, Maine, called The Holy Donut. This story is about my experience of starting a donut business to satisfy a heavy donut craving and to follow the path of finding peace with food. I needed donuts to pay my bills but also to soothe my inner critic of food restriction and learn to make peace with my body. I approached the business and my cravings with love, and the business (in six years) has blossomed from making twelve donuts a day in a pot on my stove for $5/day to an eighty-employee, $6 million/year operation.

This book is dedicated to my dad! I am enjoying a wonderful life and thank him for his help and wisdom to get me here.

I'd also like to acknowledge my family: Liz, Cynthia (my mom) and Jeff Buckwalter for helping make the business work so well.

Leigh Kellis

Donuts

Donuts

Donuts changed my life.

I decided to make donuts after years of telling myself I couldn't have them, and instead listening to another voice that said,

"Yes, you can."

This book is the story of making a business—and all decisions—out of love.

Donuts were love for my appetite. Love for my cravings. Love for my community. Love for my life—needing to pay my bills. Love for my family. Love for my daughter. My dad's love for me.

Chapter 1

The Story

I n 2009 I went through a divorce. Like anyone who's gone through it knows, it can leave you ravaged and exhausted. I felt hollow. I was living in my parents' attic, as I'd taken refuge there once I realized my marriage was beyond repair. I didn't explain and didn't know how to explain anything to my six-year-old daughter at the time. I said, "We're just going to sleep at your grandparents' house —forever!" We stayed in their unheated attic room for ten months. I remember feeling a complicated mix of relief and freedom, and then despair (for my daughter's sake) and guilt. I was happy to be on my own but consumed with angst that she would now be from a broken home. Because both my ex-husband and I came from divorce (my parents were divorced, but roommates at the time we lived in their attic), we always said our child would never be the product of a broken home. Then it broke.

I drifted in the attic life for months. It was cold and I kept it messy, as my head was really unclear. At one point my mom was beside herself. She'd had it with my drifting. She sat me down and said, "You need to get a life."

I said, "I know. I'm trying." The only thing I could really think about was soothing the pain. I wanted to go out, drink wine, and find a boyfriend. I really wanted to distract myself and not think about the confusion my daughter was going through. I couldn't bear it. The confusion was due to her being forced to go back and forth between her dad and me and our weird, temporary living situations (he was renting a room at an acquaintance's house, and I was in the attic). So she was in purgatory. And I still didn't explain much to her; I didn't have the words. We shuffled her around, as I tried to make some money while surviving the attic. And when she was with her dad, I'd go on dates. Then I met someone.

While we were living in the attic, I got a job at a wine bar. It was dreamy to me because I love wine bars, and the owner was someone who had caught my eye in town years prior. He was opening a tiny, hole-in-the-wall, Italian wine bar that grabbed my attention because to me anything involving wine and socializing was appealing. The place had an all-Italian wine theme, so I knew it would provide a good dose of soul that I needed. He styled the place in a very artful and creative way that was cool. I knew I wanted to spend time there. And I needed to make money.

It took about three weeks before we were dating. He was very intriguing to me, with tons of ambition and good taste. He'd built the wine bar, and it was perfect and tasteful and quirky. I ran the twenty-seat place like it was my home. I loved it. It was a source of easy and fun money.

I went into work three nights a week, and I was always jittery about seeing him. After nine years of marriage, I liked the butterflies of a new relationship. He was quick to ask me over after work for a ridiculously good bottle of wine and something outrageously delicious that he was cooking up. My marriage hadn't ever been focused on pleasure so much; we'd focused mostly on practical things—renovating our house, saving money, and *not* going out to dinner. I, being someone with a very needy soul, was starving for pleasure, good food, and good wine, and I didn't realize how deep the deficit was until I was out of it. Now suddenly, I was exposed to someone (my wine bar boss) saying, "Here, have this amazing glass of wine, and let's go out for three-hundred-dollar dinner after." My heart, stomach, and entire being were rejoicing to have met this person who gave me permission and encouragement to indulge. I was the perfect candidate; I was dying for it.

Throughout this relationship with my boss, we did some traveling. For some reason, my main mission on several of our trips became to find a good local donut shop. It was a bit of an obsession, and it makes sense now, as it correlated perfectly with the new "permission" I had to eat whatever the hell I wanted with him. I had been a food restrictor for a long time, hyperaware of eating the wrong things and afraid of gaining weight. I had always loved donuts but hadn't eaten them for a long time.

We found a couple good donut shops in Boston and San Francisco, but nothing that satisfied my requirements for a donut that was good quality and totally hit the pleasure button. I found an old-school place in Boston that had tasty but not great quality donuts. I liked an "organic donut" in San Francisco that excited me because I thought it was sort of healthier. It triggered a lightbulb—ooh, quality donuts. Cool concept! And I enjoyed a few, but they weren't exceptionally scrumptious. I also found some packaged donuts in health food stores that were labeled organic or gluten free. They were definitely edible and satisfying, but they were frozen or packaged. The thought, though, was born to combine good ingredients and good donuts in one. Then people like me, who are neurotic but love and need donuts and flavor, could have their donut needs met.

A few months later we were sitting at a restaurant eating an indulgent dinner and probably on our second bottle of wine, and he said, "You should open a donut shop."

It was a radical concept at that moment. It resonated with me deeply, I took it in for about three seconds and got a yes in my core. Yes, that needed to happen. No, I had no idea how to do anything related to starting a business, but I knew I wanted a donut shop. In that moment I saw it. I felt like I could stop floundering in life; I just needed to make donuts. It excited me head to toe. I needed it for myself, and I could see instantaneously that the world—my town—needed a donut shop. And it wasn't because Portland, Maine, needed more food options. We had plenty. We needed something we didn't have—that old-school, nostalgic comfort of simpler times ... the smell of deep-fried donuts and cinnamon, and the way you feel when you walk into a donut shop and get excited and hyped for something sweet and soothing. This is a feeling you don't get from a bakery with bread and croissants (although I love bakeries in general). There's an anticipation with donuts that I love—the fat! It's deeply satisfying. I don't want a muffin! I wanted fat … dough deep fried … perfectly sweet … a little crispy, and soft on the inside … the right amount of cinnamon. It had to happen! I needed it. I knew other people needed it.

He suggested I open a shop, and my gears started turning. I started the next day. I was all in.

I went to a bookstore and wrote down every recipe I could find. I didn't want to buy cookbooks; I just wanted to jot down some recipes and go home and attempt to make donuts. I gathered recipes, some with sour cream, some with potatoes, some with yeast. I had the basics at home already—flour, eggs, sugar, salt, and baking powder. I had to get buttermilk, vanilla, and powdered sugar. The research and development phase was cheap and low-commitment, which is what I wanted. I didn't want to spend money on this fantasy. Yet.

I practiced and fumbled through several recipes. I made lots of duds for a couple weeks. I brought samples into his bar, where I still worked. I shared the samples with crazed enthusiasm despite the fact that they were only mediocre. I was charged at the thought of homemade donuts. But the sour cream donuts were boring. The other recipes were dry. Then I made a recipe from *The Joy of Cooking* (Irma Rombauer, Marion Rombauer Becker & Ethan Becker) cookbook: potato donuts with no yeast. They were stellar. I loved the texture … soft and pillowy … kind of the like fried dough I got at the fair as a kid … nice and satisfying but not greasy … the perfect nuance of nutmeg and a crispy edge. I called my neighbor Zeile and my dad and said, "Come over. You need to try this." I tossed the little babies in powdered sugar and cinnamon and felt like I had hit on donut magic.

I made them a couple more days and then thought, *I need to get these out there into the world.* The dream of the donut shop (someday) was hanging in the air, and I knew some market testing was necessary. I took a plate of donuts to my local coffee shop and said, "Please eat these." And "Will you sell them?" She said, "Sure!"

I was nervous! I felt like this donut thing was my mission in life, and I wanted to execute it properly. That said, I executed my business in a very casual, unconventional way. I took a plate of homemade donuts to a local shop. I knew no other way to launch a business. I rarely plan ahead—I just leap. I knew I wanted a product that I loved, which was the case. I loved these donuts. I had no business plan or real clue on how to sell a product to "real businesses" in the community, but I decided to wing it and let the donuts speak for themselves. I just wanted people to get them in their mouths ...

I was making twelve donuts a day in a pot on my stove. I hiked down the hill daily to deliver to the one coffee shop. I would be so nervous every time I delivered. *Are the donuts cooked through?* (I was making them in a pot with a thermometer, and the temperature went all over the place ... 375 degrees one minute, then way up or down the next minute. It was hard to control the oil on the stove.) *Will people buy them today? Do people think I'm ridiculous for now being the "donut delivery girl"? Can I really do this every day? Is five dollars a dozen per day worth my while to get out of bed at 5 a.m., seven days a week?*

Then I brought them everywhere, and the wholesale business grew. I still was going on complete razor focus. I never questioned the mission. I felt fully that making donuts was my mission in life. With most creative projects in the history of my life, I would lose steam and inspiration after that initial crazed excitement about something. With donuts, the energy never waned. I wanted to bring donuts to the people come hell or high water. It was a relentless drive.

The wholesale business grew, and I quickly secured about eight more cafes that agreed to sell my donuts. I was soon renting a kitchen space in my friend's restaurant at 5 a.m. every morning. He served just dinner, so the unoccupied kitchen space was perfect for me to rent in the mornings. I was able to work in a real kitchen so I was certified to sell publicly.

I was selling a few dozen dozens per week. Whole Foods agreed to sell them, as did our local coffee roaster, who had five locations, so I felt legitimate in my endeavors. Each place (except Whole Foods) was selling only one dozen each per day … so it was a lot of running around. But I felt great and validated that people wanted the product and were buying them every day. I graduated to a small countertop fryer, making four donuts at a time, and the fryer had temperature control and a timer, so I felt like a real pro! I still was making them four at a time, so when my wholesale orders grew to ten dozen a day and then more, it was taking me hours to cut, shape, and fry them all. Admittedly, it was a horribly inefficient and amateurish way to make them for a wholesale business, but I didn't know better and didn't have the ability or space to buy a big fryer. I made them in this small-scale way for ten months. The wholesale operation grew in this rented kitchen space to one hundred dozen per week. I eventually bought a second small fryer, so I doubled my capacity to making eight donuts at a time. In retrospect, I can smile at my commitment to producing the product seven days a week, even if it was in the most glacial, inefficient, and exhausting way possible. Hindsight is always 20/20.

Four months into the ten months of wholesale-only business, my dad told me he'd be there at 6 a.m. the next day to help me. He said, "You have a business on your hands, and you can't afford to pay anyone."

I said, "Okay." But I didn't want help. I liked working alone, and I had just gone through a divorce and wanted to control the whole situation. I didn't want a man telling me I couldn't do something on my own, and I wanted to do it alone. I was finding my feet in my life. I also didn't want to talk to anyone at 6 a.m. But he showed up. And he ran around the kitchen doing anything I needed and fumbled through cutting donuts and shaping them and handing me trays to fry eight at a time. I fried feverishly because it was a slow process and I wanted to get all these dozens out to the coffee shops by 7 a.m., at opening time. I always felt tons of anxiety about getting it all done by 7 a.m. I was a ball of nerves about "doing it all right." My dad would grab all the bins of donuts, each labeled for each shop around town. He'd always be so chipper and positive! And I was an emotional wreck every day. I fried them as fast as I could, and he'd load up the car and speed around town. Then he'd come back for any that I couldn't get ready by 7 a.m.

I remember being such a bitch. I took it very seriously that my product was "public," and I wanted everything to be perfect every day. Usually, the last people we can hide emotions from are our parents. I was nervous and anxious and I was often overbearing with my dad, but he took it in stride. He delivered the donuts every single day and never reacted to my insanity. He became my right-hand man, and he was fully on board to help me open a shop of my own when we were ready. He was committed to helping me because that's what good dads do. They support their kids.

In fall 2011 we started to think about getting out of the rented kitchen space and looking for commercial space to open the shop. A realtor gave us the tour around town of available spaces. One came up that initially felt totally wrong ... then something about it felt right. It was quirky and out of the way of any other shops. It was a stand-alone building that suddenly struck me as the perfect place for a neighborhood donut shop. Off the beaten path, it was an old asymmetrical building that used to be a garage. It had all the character we needed, as well as a walk-in cooler and a ventilation system we required. We signed the lease.

My mom loaned us a little money when banks wouldn't give us the time of day.

We had no idea what we were doing; we'd never run a bakery. I had no business experience. We threw the place together. I did all the painting, and my dad built the service counter by taking apart the existing one and restructuring it. I had no idea what I was in for.

We opened in March 2012. We had a steady trickle of customers for the first couple weeks. Then the local newspaper wrote about us, and the people lined up. I was flipping donuts on day 12 of our being open, and the line was out the door. My dad was shaping donuts next to me to put on the screen for me to lower into the oil, and I said, "Don't turn around." The line of people terrified me. I couldn't make donuts fast enough. My anxiety was full-blown from this point on. I wanted the product to be perfect, but that was hard to achieve with our lack of experience in making a handmade product at such high volume. A line out the door meant people had high expectations ... and I was the only donut maker at this point. I was on autopilot: Wake up in the morning, cut the dough, fry it, glaze it, sell it, clean up, make dough for the next day, buy more ingredients. Make enough for the masses. Figure out how to run a business. Figure out how to work with my father every day. Do it seven days a week. Keep it going. There was no turning back.

I called my old wine bar boss this first really busy weekend that second or third week. I said, "I made 1000 donuts today. And it wasn't enough. I couldn't keep up, and I don't know what I'm doing. It's overwhelming."

He said, "You'd better figure it out. You're going to piss off your customers." I was terrified and charged. I knew he was right. I had to figure it out. It took a few years past that point for me to really understand how to meet demand ... but it did happen.

A year and a half later my brother-in-law, Jeff, jumped in. He quit his job and put all his cards (so to speak) on the donut business. He said, "We can make this into a multimillion-dollar business." I said okay. I was clueless. I was just trying to keep the routine going every day. He saw something that I didn't, and we decided to open a second location. Another commercial space was secured, and we went for it. This was our second opening with minimal funding. We pulled it together, friends painted, we gathered equipment, and it seemed reasonable to open another location across town given the success of the first location. We were naïve in so many ways, but the momentum of the business was powerful. The second location was expensive, but the customers showed up. It was a great move.

We rolled along for two years, making these two shops work. We increased profitability, and my brother-in-law brought tons of structure and order to the business that my dad and I never had. My dad and I went full steam every day attending to the many more practical details the business required: making and selling donuts ... hiring people ... cleaning the place ... running around buying supplies ... fixing equipment. Jeff helped organize the business from another angle. He saw it from above. He saw the bigger picture. He looked at the finances (not my strong point). He got rid of people who didn't fit with us anymore, and he found the right people to manage effectively. And thank God, he brought a perspective that helped the business be ready for the next level of expansion.

In April 2017 we opened a big, third location with a drive-thru in a highly visible location on Route 1. I had resisted this expansion for three years. So many people said, "Open more locations! Franchise! When are you opening a third location?" I wasn't ready, and I was terrified of losing the soul of the business. I thought more locations would mean we'd be diluting the specialness of the business somehow. Then we looked at a Tim Horton's building that had been vacated. The space really felt soulless. I said, "No way," when we looked at it.

Then I paused … I went home, and in my alone time, I said, "Holy Donut, what do you want to be?"

I asked the business; I got myself out of the way. It said, "I want to be bigger. I want to bring good stuff to more people. More is okay."

I felt relieved and was comforted to tune into the energy of the business. This business was founded and run in love, and *it* wanted to grow into itself and maximize its potential. The business had been conceived in my own need to honor my cravings. It had been born out of a need to do something in my life that felt positive and would contribute to our town. This business loved to bring comfort to people.

Committing to a third location felt significant. It was no longer a little mom-and-pop donut shop with casual hand-painted interiors and thrown-together aesthetics. We did the third location the right way, with a designer and a contractor and a huge bank loan. It felt like a fairy tale. I still look at the building and pinch myself. It is symbolic of a dream come true. It shows the power of manifestation and vision, the result of focused energy and good intentions. Everyone involved knows that the mission is to enrich a person's day with positive energy and spread a little love and kindness through donuts and a smile. It's not overcomplicated. It's something that happens to be needed nowadays. The sweet innocence of a donut shop is just as marketable and sellable as the donuts themselves.

So why did I need donuts so badly after the

divorce?

I needed what all women need—

Women need peace.

And flavor.

Permission to eat what we crave.

To acknowledge our desires.

To love the smell of food, pies baking, chicken

roasting, tomato sauce on the stove ... and to be

intoxicated and soothed by it.

We need to eat without hating our bodies

And give ourselves the best.

To surround ourselves with food we love,

And know when to stop.

We need a break

And ease

And comfort

And to be without guilt and preoccupation

about what we are eating while gathering with

people we love.

We need magic

And to not feel like shit.

To have something to look forward to,

Food to look forward to.

And pleasure.

We need to eat with gusto and passion like women who are *not* afraid of our appetite.

Chapter 2

What Helps

T here is a peace to be found in *eating* what you love that I haven't found in any other way. Not everyone can relate to this connection, but for me it's fully correlated. For so long I struggled with being at peace with my body that the angst manifested in my obsession with food. I wanted to "fix" my criticism of my body and my internal unease by eating better, restricting, dieting, "getting control." It's no surprise I never fixed myself by dieting. We can't be fixed by dieting. I had to start to eat with love to make any headway on my crippling anxiety. I had to eat what I loved and make peace with my cravings to address the deeper issues. For so long I struggled with what I "should eat" or "shouldn't eat." It was a wonderful way to distract myself from feeling anything else or thinking about uncomfortable topics.

Food obsession always reveals a deeper worry.

To eat in peace allows us to get honest about what we really feel. The new mantra had to become, "What would I *really* love to eat today?" I had to frame eating out of love. Restriction and control were causing me too much pain. I was constantly setting myself up for failure. "Don't eat that." And then I would, and then I would repent. Food obsession prevents a woman from really being present in her life. It is the ultimate method of avoidance. It separates us from others and from life. So asking, "What would I *really* love to eat today?" is sinking into the truer questions: What do I really want? What do I really, really want? What do I crave? What do I desire? What can I have? Can I allow myself to have it? Enjoy it?

Am I capable of allowing myself to have what I want?

These are amazing questions. They hit so deep in me. Not allowing myself to have the food I wanted was a message to myself that I didn't believe in my own desires and I certainly didn't trust myself with my appetite and needs. I feared that if I let myself eat what I really wanted, the cravings would *never* be satisfied. The cavern of desire was too deep; I would eat and eat until I blew up, because I didn't feel like I had a cutoff point. But the deep cavern of desire was not and is not and still won't ever be about food. Cliché, yes.

But the truest thing I know.

And trust. I didn't trust myself with my appetite. I remember food panic going way back to early college. I'd wake up in the morning and be stricken with anxiety. I'd start my day thinking, *I can't do this. I can't eat like a normal person. My appetite is colossal, and there's never enough.* And the resulting feeling was total despair and angst. I didn't know how to approach this with love; I just drifted through every day in anxiety and feeling bad about everything I ate.

Even now, it still feels unnatural at times. But I say, "What would I *really* love to eat today?" because I know that's how I need to talk to myself. It has to be a daily practice. It changes the brain. It rewires the thinking from, *I shouldn't. I don't trust myself. I'm a deep well of insatiable need,* to *I can give to myself. I trust myself. I can live in peace and harmony with my desires. It's all good.*

Trust Yourself

Trusting oneself feels so unnatural. It's like the fear of the beast of insatiable hunger is so much more familiar. But that's why it's so cool to look at it with a magnifying glass. Look at the fear! I am so petrified of my desires. What the hell for? What if I ate sensibly, stopped when I was full, and then sat back (while still comfortable in my body) and just allowed myself to *think*? To think about life, think about my dreams. To think about God who created me and why. What is there on the other side of fear and panic and self-doubt? Really pause and let thoughts and visions come in. Even if there is nothing there when obsession and guilt are tamed and you're just kind of neutral, there is an in-between place where you aren't obsessing or punishing yourself. Just wait; something else will come. Often when we obsess about food and our body, it's entertainment and a habitual way to keep the mind occupied. If I ate sensibly, and stopped when was full, would life be dull? Would I be bored? What would fill that space of thinking about it all? Dieting and looking ahead to "Someday when I get it right, I'll be happy" provides a nice sense of hope. It's a great way to delay peace and happiness.

Imagine cooking, preparing, and sitting down to eat with full attention. Include a candle, pretty plates, and calm surroundings. You care about yourself and the people you're cooking for. You want to spark the appetite and the senses, so enjoy smelling the garlic in the oil (which I often add to most things I make just to the get the house smelling good). I love a glass of wine while I cook, and amazing music. The result: the gift of being present. Being at home in your life and giving your needs all of your attention ... it ripples to other areas of life. I repeat:

Being at home in your life and giving your needs all of your attention ... it ripples to other areas of life.

To be in tune with eating, and being present with it, suddenly opens the mind and trains it to be present elsewhere. Sit and eat. Taste; don't rush. Resist the urge to read a magazine or eat mindlessly. Attempt to not look at the iPhone (difficult!) But give it your time; eat with awareness because you give a shit about yourself and you want to enjoy every bite ...

Acknowledge that You Have Needs.

What do you love?

Let's start with, What do you love to *eat*?

Make a list. *Surround* yourself with that list. Stock your kitchen with foods you *love*. I do.

Foods I *Adore*

Apples and chunky peanut butter

Salt and pepper potato chips

Dark chocolate cake with ganache

Sauvignon Blanc (any wine!.... more on that below)**

Whipped cream

Romaine with real Caesar dressing

Papaya

Cheeseburgers with mayo and cheddar, lettuce, tomato, and onion

Crispy homemade buffalo chicken wings

Green grapes

English breakfast tea with soymilk and honey

Blackened salmon

Rice with butter and salt

Vodka tonic and lime

Spicy pasta Alfredo

Mushrooms sautéed in garlic, butter, and wine

Bacon

Pie à la mode

Red peppers and hummus

Mayonnaise for everything

Provolone cheese

Avocados

Toast

Brussels sprouts—crispy!

Allowing yourself to have food you adore and to eat in peace brings ease to all areas of your life. To be in dissonance with your desires creates so much angst.

You can't get shit done in the world if you're struggling with your *most basic* daily needs and desires.

Women are so worried about being fat when there's so much to be done. It's a crisis and an epidemic. Food and "being fat" angst always reveals a deeper worry. Am I unlovable? Do I have any idea how it would feel to be comfortable in my body? Do I want to be in my power? Do I know how?

Eat what you *love,* and then move the hell on!! You may not know what to move on to … and that's the craziness of body angst. But when the peace with ourselves starts to become a little more natural, we can start to tune in to what we might do with our lives.

What do we do with our lives? What is the point? The point is to be at peace with yourself.

That's the point.

The world needs more women to be at peace.

Eating what you love means you can eat. Then move the hell on. There is no repenting. No guilt. No obsessing on "How can I burn this off?" No more wasted thoughts. No more wasted time. No more wasted life. Eat what you love, stop, and then get on with your life. You have shit to do! If you *don't* know what else to do with yourself, at *least* stop filling your time abusing yourself. Let's start with that and see what seeps in to the empty space. Anything can happen (thoughts, inspiration, intuition, motivation) when space is opened up to think, *feel*, and be in peace.

Imagine what would love to get your attention if you took your attention off restricting, repenting, and fixing yourself. Imagine what you could focus on if you weren't always doing damage control.

Wine

Wine is a big player on my love list.

Dear Wine,

I love you.

I remember being twenty-two and having just moved to San Francisco. I was introduced to the stimulating and arousing experience of starting to appreciate you, my dear friend. I love everything about you … the astringent effect on the tongue, the complicated aromas, the warm buzz, the association with a date in a dimly lit restaurant or with best friends—and laughter. I wish I could drink you still in mass quantity. But I got sensitive. Shit. I will never give you up entirely. I'm forced to moderate against my will. You give me great comfort and pleasure.

But I get great comfort from prayer too … so I

have to drink less. Please know that I will always

love you.

Sincerely,

Leigh

Pray more; drink less.

Order the Big Piece!

Order (or cut for yourself) the big piece of cake—or at least a normal-sized piece. We (I) often take "just a bite." Then we go back to the cake twelve times for "just *one more* bite." And then we hate ourselves. The goal is *to no longer engage in activities that result in self-hatred!* Food was not designed to inspire self-hatred. If something is causing self-hatred, you have a real opportunity to take a look. Order the normal-sized (or big!) piece. Enjoy every morsel. Give it to yourself without condition. This is so hard sometimes, to enjoy something fully without the chaos of voices in the head: *You're really going to eat the* whole *piece? Just eat half. You* really *shouldn't have eaten that.*

Giving yourself the whole piece is sanity. Going back for "one more bite" twelve times because you weren't satisfied the first time is not sanity. Make sanity your priority. Sanity and peace are the new goals.

Feeling at peace with food is *gold* when so many things in life are not peaceful … or satisfying.

Pie Ritual (Self-Love through Pie!)

I have a new ritual. I buy a pie every week. I keep in on the counter. I have a nice, luscious piece every day. One piece à la mode. And, my God, do I *look forward* to that every day! Usually I eat it alone. It's my indulgence. And there's no guilt. I look at it throughout the day with excitement and love.

I get to have that! It's something to look forward to!

We all need something to look forward to, even if it's a piece of pie. Some people may not know the significance of this permission, but it's powerful and symbolic and deeply effective to make peace with food and cravings and needs. The pie needs to be there. Available. And no, you won't eat the whole thing at once, because you are allowing yourself to eat one wonderful piece every day right when you're craving—and you're going to enjoy the fuck out of it. I eat it in peace, my eyes closed if necessary. I eat it quietly, with attention. I try not to stare at my iPhone.

Body

I want nothing more than to be at peace in my body.

And it's been a work in progress forever. Then recently I gained a whole bunch of weight. Mysteriously. My body just changed. I thought, *What the hell just happened? I've been the same weight for so many years, and now I'm twenty pounds heavier?* I was surprised by my reaction—I did not respond in guilt and torture and shame. I went to the doctor to see if there was a medical reason (no). Then I said to myself, *Okay, I'm listening.* Radical.

> *Sometimes your body tells you what you think and feel*
>
> *before you have any idea what you think and feel.*

I think I was pissed … and stressed … and worried. I assume my subconscious was working overtime and my body was puffing up, and I needed to stop and assess my life. It was not that I was overeating. It wasn't about the food. I knew that. I knew that it was emotional and protective.

So I said, *I will not stop eating pie. I will not torment myself to lose this weight.*

I will listen.

I will ask

Whom do I need to forgive?

And more importantly, How can I forgive?

And why am I stressed? And pissed?

I know this is not about food. I will continue to eat with love, and I will continue to pursue forgiveness in my life.

I did some deep digging. I had been pissed all of the previous year at my daughter's father. That was no secret. He had moved to Hawaii "for better weather" and left me to be a solo parent. Part of me was happy he was gone, because it taught me indisputably that "I can do this." But the other part was pissed that I had no help raising a thirteen-year-old. And it was manifesting in my body. Then came the kicker: I realized I didn't know how to forgive. It didn't feel easy. I felt stuck. So I just kept asking, How can I forgive? If I knew the way, what would it look like? Then it came to me. It wasn't all about him. It was about me. I had chosen him. I had chosen that marriage. And I was 50% of the divorce. I had chosen it all. I take responsibility. Can I forgive myself? That's my only true responsibility. So I work on that, and I work on anything that brings peace and forgiveness. And less stress. How about a massage? Or a walk? Or more sleep? Or just chilling out, going catatonic once in a while? I'm going to deal with this weird weight gain with new eyes. I'll take care of myself and stress less.

It's not about food; it's about my heart. It always was.

Don't get me wrong. I'm still pissed that he moved. A thirteen-year-old girl needs her father. But it is what it is. I focus on my job—being a mother. And I am still working like crazy at forgiveness of him.

I looked at myself with compassion too. My father was sick with cancer. And he wasn't likely to get better. I was worried. And sad. And I realized (for me) that the opposite of fat is faith.

I may have gained weight because of pure unfamiliar emotions. My dad was really ill (more on that later), and I was "bracing for impact," building a protective layer. I had to have faith that I would survive both solo parenting and my dad dying...

I did something else radical. After many years of jogging constantly, I said to myself, Just stop. Stop jogging. Stop! Enough is enough. It had been a daily attempt to sweat, get endorphins, fix my mood, feel better, feel okay, and "work on" my body. I felt it was time to pause. I had been so desperate to "feel okay" every day … and I did after jogging, but the angst would start all over again the next day. The endorphins certainly don't last; I'd need a fix the next day, so I knew something wasn't right. I had to see what was under the surface. I needed to stop (literally) running from what I was feeling and *settle in.*

I had to settle in to myself! In stillness. The jogging was no longer making me feel okay. I didn't feel okay. I was pissed and stressed and worried and sad, and I had to feel those things. I took a risk—*no more jogging.*

I had many fears:

I will never move again.

I will never get off the couch.

I will balloon to four hundred pounds.

I will never stop eating.

I will hate myself.

I will give up hope.

I will suffocate in a quagmire of sadness.

My life and all momentum will come to a screeching halt, and I'll be humongous and sedentary and unmotivated.

Then suddenly a couple months had gone by, and none of those fears had come true. I didn't lose all the weight, but I didn't gain any either. I felt happier and calmer. I walked. I looked around. I listened to books on tape about God and life and women. I cried about my father. I got peace from walking and listening to inspiring words in my headphones, which I had never got from jogging. I got soul soothing, and I relaxed in a way I'd never relaxed before. The haunting voice saying to *go jogging* was gone. That little critical beast lost its power.

Not that criticism ever goes away. We can't really talk about our bodies without addressing the inner criticism.

Goal: crucify ourselves less.

Practice: look at other women. In your mind tell them, *You look good! You're doing the best you can!* I do this. It helps reverse the constant ticker of criticism that lives in my head.

Practice thinking in love toward yourself and other women. It's a practice. Lord knows, it's not automatic or habitual or familiar. But it's so worth the practice.

The truth is that we all have the same basic commonalities.

All women want to give.

And connect.

To *create* (anything!)

To live well.

To have purpose.

To taste, feel, nurture, and heal.

To not hate our bodies.

To be appreciated.

To get shit done.

To fantasize.

To receive.

To have help.

To know when we have nothing to give.

To have meaning.

Meaning

We need meaning. What the hell is the point? What defines meaning?

The point is to be at peace with yourself.

That's the point.

I find peace through loving my body ... eating the pie without guilt ... taking a walk ... and asking over and over, How can I give?

Women need to give: to ourselves and to others. That is our basic wiring. That's where the meaning lives. Giving to ourselves and others in love leads to peace; it leads to meaning.

God, please use me for love.

Perfection

Nothing disrupts inner peace like this list most of us carry in our heads:

Be perfect.

Have great hair.

Be a great mom!

Don't be a bitch.

Say the right thing.

Don't be too loud.

Don't be awkward.

Exercise.

Don't be frumpy.

Have the right clothes.

Don't scream at your kids.

Don't have road rage.

Eat right! (Vegan? Gluten-free? Act like you don't care?)

Don't be fat.

Don't screw up your relationships.

Don't wear white after Labor Day.

Have an amazing career.

No pressure.

Maybe pick one or two of these goals. But the whole relentless list is a little exhausting whether we realize or not the expectations we have of ourselves. Pursue inner peace like it's your job.

Mantra: I attract and welcome anyone and anything that contributes to my inner peace.

Chapter 3

Thoughts

Worry

Worry. Worry. Worry.

Women worry.

We worry because we care. We care so much that the worry festers in the back of our minds all day.

Things I need to worry about:

> My kid
>
> My well-being
>
> Paying my bills
>
> My own inner peace
>
> Getting enough sleep
>
> How I treat myself and others
>
> What kind of pie I want this week

Things I don't need to worry about:

> Everyone else's happiness
>
> People liking me

The rain forests

The most recent earthquake in South America or terrorist attack in Europe (worrying doesn't change anything)

All of the planet

Humanity

Everything

I always worry about everyone else's happiness. I realized this is kind of (you think?) tiring.

Each person's life (and happiness) is between him or her and God.

Not my business. Phew! Off the hook.

Silence

Silence is another factor in peace. Silence. I need so much of it lately.

The less I say, the happier I am!

Note to self: it's okay to shut up. Be quiet and listen for what you love, what you need, and what you want. There is so much noise these days. How can we hear anything if there is never silence? I pursue silence like it's gold.

I sing more and talk less. I listen to music like it's a drug. I need it; whatever soothes the soul, put it in your life… music, lilies, friends who make you laugh, the beach, baths, as much wine as you can handle without feeling crappy.

Sadness

It occurred to me I have been subconsciously dodging sadness my whole life. It's always been there. Food obsession was a wonderful drug, a way to avoid sadness. If a woman is thinking about what to eat, what not to eat, how to perfect the body, and berating herself in the process, it occupies the mind and keeps sadness and uncomfortable feelings at bay. But exchanging one set of uncomfortable feelings (food/body obsession) for another (sadness) is not helpful. The food insanity was initially constructed to protect myself, but it became too painful. It was time to get honest and realize:

All women have sadness.

Stop pretending like it's not fucking there!

It's not a defect.

It's a sign of your big, huge heart. You're sad because you care and you're human, and most of us will do *anything* to avoid feeling it. We numb ourselves with food ... hate ourselves ...

shop ourselves into debt (please, God, help me stop buying stupid shit).

Be sad sometimes.

Please *cry*

Ignoring it doesn't make it go away.

Thank yourself for your big, beautiful heart.

Sadness can be so vague. There's not always a clear root. Life is temporary; it ends. We fall in love with the people in our lives, and then we all die.

Life is both beautiful and sad at all times.

Of course we feel it.

The bravest (and sometimes most excruciating) thing a woman can do is feel what she feels.

Relationships

I love men. I do. I have had many boyfriends and a husband. At this point (at least temporarily) I love being alone; I like to sleep alone, wake up alone, cook alone, eat alone, walk alone, sit in a café and watch people alone. I don't mind solitude one bit. I like being with a companion sometimes, but currently my focus is on *getting right* with *myself*.

That's what really excites the hell out of me—making peace with myself.

Reality Check

Yes, these are first-world problems. I have a deep understanding that many women around the world don't have the luxury of needing to make peace with pie and donuts. There are larger issues of safety and survival across the planet, and people are starving. In our country, we have abundance, thank the Lord. And we struggle with ourselves in ways many other women don't. I have compassion for all women, and I pray for women who have challenging lives. The goal, though, is to improve life for all of us, however that looks in each culture. In our culture we desperately need more love, more self-acceptance, and more connection with ourselves. The effects of this elevated thinking will be felt around the world. Every woman anywhere who grows into peace with herself is a huge bonus for everyone. The world *needs* women to be dwelling in peace.

Declaration

I will be grateful for my life.

I will live with flavor.

I will listen to my cravings.

I will not stuff myself.

I will not be cruel to myself.

I will honor my appetite.

I will feel what I feel.

I will be psyched that I have soul and passion and taste buds and a healthy body.

I will acknowledge that I want to have a good life.

I will not stop eating pie.

I will enjoy every bite.

I will not guilt-trip myself or others.

I will not promise myself I'll go running tomorrow to make up for eating.

I will spend time with men who love to eat and love me and my body and give me immense support.

I will make feeling awesome my top priority.

Chapter 4

Being Thirteen

T o my daughter ...

What a massive and important responsibility I have! I need to raise a daughter in this confusing day and age, to become a happy, effective, grounded woman. Whoa! What a task.

The goal is to raise a girl who likes herself.

So you're thirteen ...

You're curious.

You're insecure.

You want friends (and they want you).

You want a good life.

You want to like your body.

You have voices in your head saying that you don't measure up.

You want boys to think you're beautiful.

You want to feel beautiful. (And you should! You're wired to want to feel beautiful. Embrace this.)

You want good hair, good nails, and good clothes. All good. Have them.

Start asking yourself *now, What do I love?*

Set love as your guiding principle now.

I wish I had been given this advice … to excavate early on the deep desires. What excites you? Travel? Horses? Children? Oceanography? Food? Nature? Fashion? What excites you? How can you use that as a barometer for all choices in your life?

How can you start now to set love *as the tone for your life?*

How can you be happy? How can you feel satisfied? I know you'll want something deeper; you'll want to feel connection and meaning. I know because I've been there.

Smile at other girls.

Pray for other girls around the world with difficult lives.

Realize and *know* that other girls are just like you and want the same things.

You *all* need

Compassion (every girl goes through hell; we all have

scars, pain, and deep challenges)

To get through the day

To like yourselves

To feel okay

To like how you look in jeans

To not be embarrassed

To not hate your bodies

To deal with your parents (some are good; some are

awful)

To feel smart

To love your life

To feel purpose

To feel hope

To feel noticed

To be respected

To have dreams

To not feel scared of the world

To believe in good men

To feel like there's a point

The point? To be thirteen. To be in wonder! To live! To enjoy your life! To be at peace ... open yourself up to wonder.

Think about your amazing self. You didn't create yourself (thought-provoking). Be curious. God wants you here. You have this magnificent body, eyes that see, and a heart that works like a machine without your help. It's not plugged into anything! You have a body that heals itself. You are a magical creature. Say thank you to God. Talk to God. Be curious about God/a higher power/universal intelligence ... whatever you want to call it. Be proud of your questions; be open to talking about deep things. Females need depth and spirit and faith.

Be all of it*!*

Be deep and soulful! AND beautiful *and* put together!

Wear lip gloss.

Think.

Pray.

Be human.

Buy only the jeans that make you feel awesome.

Watch birds and clouds, and appreciate nature.

Do your nails.

Count your blessings.

Talk nicely about yourself (practice!)

Be vulnerable; you *have* to ask for help. People want to help you.

Ask questions.

Seek wisdom—talk to people who have "been there."

Listen to what they say.

Watch an inspiring movie.

Watch a stupid movie.

Enjoy your own company—spend time alone.

Save some money—even a dollar a week.

Attend to yourself inside and out.

Be a good friend.

Don't neglect your soul.

Say thank you to God.

That's where the fun begins—asking now. (Don't wait until you're forty! Please!)

What do I love?

What do I care about?

What do I love to do?

Ask daily. And ask, what would I love to *eat* today?

Listen to your body. Is it chips? Salad? Cucumbers? Ice cream? Avocados? Listening to your body is a challenge. Start now. This is the time when the detachment can happen …

Stay with yourself.

Things can get rocky. It's *not* unusual to start feeling disconnected from yourself, disconnected from your body and your cravings … what you want versus what you think you "should want." Food, life, adventure. What do *you* really want?

And then there's always the preoccupation of *How does this guy feel about me?* It will distract you as you are figuring out what you are, what you need, and what you feel. It can become more important than *How do I feel about me?*

This will be your greatest challenge.

Guys.

Seeing your own life through your *own* lens and not the lens of the guy in your Spanish class …

This will be your greatest challenge.

What do I love?

Ask!

Don't wait until you're forty—or fifty or sixty—to ask yourself what you love. Don't wait!

Stay with yourself and ask what you yourself need. Know it, and at least ponder ...

The goal is to make decisions out of love, starting sooner rather than later.

The best part it's easy to obsess about what everyone else thinks. It's easy to worry that everyone is analyzing your every move.

News Flash!

No one cares.

No one is thinking about you.

You're *free*!

You're free to live a life you *love*. This is great news. Most of us women never sink into this fact!

Pray

Pray for help. Sometimes life sucks.

School sucks.

Feeling insecure sucks.

Getting out of bed early sucks.

Watching the news sucks.

Feeling left out and unpopular sucks.

Doubting yourself sucks.

Pray for help and motivation and to get out of bed every day and put your best foot forward.

Pray to not be discouraged by all the things that suck in life.

Pray for inspiration.

Pray for hope.

Femininity—Good Stuff!

Embrace your femininity. Acknowledge the beauty and fun that lives in the energy of being female:

High heels

Hair that smells good

Soft voice

Soft eyes

Appreciation for beauty and creativity

A *crazy* big heart

Fierce protective instincts

Fierce mothering abilities

Fierce pain tolerance

Fierce ability to deal with shitty situations

Compassion and wild intuition

Strength of steel

Brilliant multitasking ability

This is you.

Last but not least ...

Life 101: my mother's favorite wisdom to me:

Enjoy your life.

Enjoy your life.

Your only job is to ...

Enjoy your life, sweetie.

Chapter 5

Being Forty-Two

A friend and I were talking recently. She's forty-four. She said, *"Why is this not getting easier?"*

Yeah. I know.

Why at this age I am still struggling to like my body and not obsess about my weight.

Sighhh ...

We all feel this way. We all have lived years (a lifetime?) of body angst. It doesn't just "go away." It's a work in progress. And I'm not willing to *not* try. I will not live without effort to be good to myself, and I will be happy for any progress I make.

It is not an option to be at war with myself for a lifetime.

It is *not an option.*

I do not want to clip my own wings.

So the quest continues. Eat what you love, and the peace will follow. For many of us, it's been a lifetime of being hard on ourselves. It does not just go away.

There is no guarantee of a fairy tale ending. There will not be one day when everything "makes sense." At least let's not be at war with ourselves the short precious time that we have.

Food Angels

Call on food angels if necessary.

Not everyone needs this help! But we can't make peace with ourselves after a lifetime of torment without a little cosmic help. Ask for help when you're sad and just want to eat. Ask for help when you want to eat beyond being full and know you should stop so you don't feel sick. Sometimes you just don't know how to feel okay. Ask for help.

My peace comes from settling into my body and listening to it. This is not everyone's path to God, but this is all I know. This quest has lasted my whole adult life, and I get giddy as I feel myself finding peace with my body and with myself. Getting closer to God (being clear, being at ease, feeling faith) is a pretty good prize.

After living so long in chaos and struggle with food, the opposite certainly does feel like God.

Wisdom at Thirteen or Forty-Two Years Old

Trust where we are now, at 13, at 42, at every age…

Where you are *now* is exactly where you *should* be.

You are doing what you are meant to be doing *now*.

You know what you should know.

Your unanswered questions are okay.

Your timing is perfect.

Your lessons are right on track.

You are not behind.

Your progress is fine.

Your past struggle with yourself is okay—forgive yourself. It got you here.

Your current "imperfection" is great.

Chapter 6

Dad

T his story of love would not be complete without a section on my dad.

As I write this, he is suffering severely with pancreatic cancer. He was diagnosed in 2015 at stage 4 and proceeded to hit it hard with chemo. The emotion I have been protecting my heart from my whole life is suddenly right in front of me. Reality ... people die. Life is painful, uncomfortable, and temporary. People suffer. He, like everyone who has had to endure chemo, has been really affected and sick and exhausted all the time. He's powered through it for two years, helping in the business daily despite his feeling profoundly nauseous and horrible. Every week he would retreat, and we wouldn't see him for a day or two when the side effects were overwhelming. He'd just hide out at home, in bed, and we wouldn't hear from him. But he never complained. Never. He'd bounce back every time and show up at the donut shop with a hat on (to cover up the hair loss) and continue to be the "happy donut guy" whom everyone had been used to over the years, selling donuts and being incredibly jovial with customers. I was amazed at his stamina through the chemo process. Most people don't tolerate extreme discomfort very well, let alone continue to work like a dog.

Since the beginning of the business way back in the rented restaurant space, my dad has contributed because he has felt compelled to. He wasn't paid. He did what good dads do. They help their kids and make sure they are "good to go." He has been hell-bent on seeing that this business is a success so that his kids are taken care of. He always has had the energy to be kind to everyone in his path and the willingness to do whatever needed to be done.

When I was a kid, my dad was so steady. My parents were divorced, and both of them, although apart, were equally present and positive. My dad, in retrospect, was a true enigma. He was unfaltering in his commitment. He happened to be a bachelor when my sister and I were kids (my parents remarried each other when I was older). He'd bomb us around in the back of his van, never missing his time with us a few nights per week. And he was always patient and even-keeled. I say he was an enigma because he never imposed any of his shit on us. Like most adults, he was probably quietly preoccupied with his own stuff, figuring out life and divorce, running his business, and navigating how to be a solo dad to two girls. But he always put his best foot forward with us. He was calm, wise, and generous. Always.

In the donut business he'd been the guy I called when a counter staff person called in sick. "Dad, can you be here in ten minutes and sell donuts for eight hours?" Or our wholesale delivery guy couldn't run a delivery, and I'd call my dad and say we need you "literally right *now* to come to the shop and pick up an order for delivery. Help!" And he'd be there—100 percent of the time. Or the walk-in cooler would break, with water leaking everywhere. And I'd call my dad. "Dad, help! Fix it! Please. Thank you."

The past couple months he's been too ill to participate in the business. He's been home most of the time feeling sluggish and totally low-energy. He stopped being able to tolerate chemo. And then in the past three months, he lost the ability to eat. His stomach can't handle food, as the pancreatic cancer is too imposing. He has been on a feeding tube. He can still get around the house and have a somewhat normal life; he just has had to navigate with his feeding tube setup. The food part of his life changed dramatically. Here's this guy who loves food. We all do. Our family is (as one can imagine) quite food-centric. My mom cooks, we are in the food business, and we all love cocktails; it's just what we do, we eat and drink. So when my dad lost his tolerance for food recently, it's been tragic and, quite frankly, beyond sad to see him go through it. He's handled it with astounding grace, though, seeming almost unaffected. I said, "How can you exist without tasting? No more eating?" I'm not exaggerating. I've said, "I don't know if I'd have the will to go on. Life without food to me seems dismal and empty and not worth living."

He said, "I'm okay."

One day during his experience recently, it hit me. I said to myself, *I've been talking about food issues for so long. Trying to make peace with food … and my body … and myself and my life for so long. This is crazy. It's no longer appropriate for me to ever feel an ounce of angst around food. My father can no longer enjoy the pleasure of even a single bite.*

In his honor, I vow to eat in peace for the rest of my life.

My quest to eat in peace is now for my own growth and to respect the fact that I have the privilege of health and appetite and a stomach that works. And for him. I've watched him sit in his chair the past few months while the rest of us inhale my mother's cooking … meatballs, pasta, salad, dessert. All oohing and ahhing as we do. Pouring more wine ... going back for seconds. And my dad just sits there, talking and joking with us but not eating. He's been like a Buddha. Not complaining. And I pray for continued strength to eat in my life in peace ... and gratitude ... and appreciation that I *can* eat, and taste and digest and be alive and well.

The last few months my dad and I have had some amazing conversations. We started talking about his death. These have been some of the most uncomfortable yet honest and beautiful conversations of my life. Talking to someone you love and preparing for them to be gone is not familiar subject matter. He asked me to find music for his funeral and told me of the venues he'd lined up for the events. He planned everything because he had a vision for his services, and maybe he didn't want us to have to deal with it. We've talked about the location, the guy he has lined up to facilitate the funeral, the food—he specified chicken and haddock would be a nice menu for after the funeral! And we're talking about it, and I'm thinking, *Okay, and you won't be there. This is surreal and sad ... and unimaginable.*

I'm not sure how to approach death head-on. It's just not something we get to practice much—watching someone die slowly and attempting to prepare.

How do you know when you've loved enough?

How do you know when you've said enough? You do not. None of us really can prepare. People lose each other all the time. I love that I've had time to be with him wholeheartedly in this process. I love that I can still tell him thank you for so much. Thanks for being the perfect example of a dad. It's really cool that we got to be business partners for the last six years. I was not perfect, and we made plenty of mistakes and disagreed at times, but it was precious. We experienced things a lot of grown women and their dads never do.

I said, as I told him about this book, "I'm anxious about it. It's possible no one will get my book, that no one will understand what I'm talking about or why I wrote it."

He said, "Nope … doesn't matter. You aren't writing for them. You're writing it for you."

So, yes, I needed donuts. I needed donuts to give me a job and an income. And I just wanted to eat them without crucifying myself. What I got was much more—a realization that life responds in kind when we follow our cravings. I was craving donuts and sweet permission to let go. I had to allow myself to eat donuts, and I wanted to bring this comfort to the world. I saw love flood the business in the form of my family jumping in and great employees gravitating to us. I still see customers give us ample business to thrive and plenty of positive reinforcement to keep the momentum going. I often stand in any of our donut shops and I feel so much love for the business, it feels like being in love with a person. I see life has given me so many gifts, and I've felt my dad's love in action over the past six years. I gave to life what I truly needed to get (flavor, hard work, and the quest for inner peace and self-acceptance). In turn, life has given back to me—a hundredfold.

Saying Goodbye

M y dad died. I was so lucky to have had a dad for forty-two years who was calm, wise, and helpful. We were blessed with a full few months with him as he edged toward death to spend time, talk, ask questions, laugh, and have closure. He spent most of his decline at home, knowing death was near. Toward the end, he sat while I visited and said something so simple, "When things are good, let them be good." This hit home, it's so easy to create problems, to lose our inner peace to internal angst. He meant to remind me that most of life is just fine. Let it be.

He'd had full control of his survival, as using the feeding tube was a daily decision he was making to stay alive. One day he said, "I'm ready."

My mom called me and said, "Dad's ready, and there's a bed that just opened up today at hospice."

I burst into tears and said, "I'll be right over."

It was the most bizarre and out-of-body experience possible. I drove to my parents' house to meet them with my sister, and we escorted my dad to hospice, to go to die. My dad walked out of the house. He was disheveled and messy and had no luggage because he wasn't going to be returning. I said, "Dad, do you really want to present yourself this way?"

He had a spaghetti pot in hand because he'd been vomiting. He said, "I don't want to look too good; they might not take me."

I started hysterically laughing, and he did too. We were howling in laughter in the driveway, but his sentiment was serious. He had made the decision that he was ready to die, and he was facing it fully. He got in the car, and we drove nearby to hospice and checked him in. He rolled into the room and remarked, "This is lovely—what a nice garden view." A graceful approach to dying is a sign of a brave and beautiful man.

We sat with him for one week. He was fully conscious when we checked him in. I sat with him alone a couple times and read everything I'd written about him, so he was fully aware of everything I felt and all the ways in which I appreciated him supporting my business and my life. I said, "You were the perfect example of a dad," and I meant it. And he heard me. One of the greatest feelings to have in life is for loved ones to know how much you love them while they are still alive. A day or two later, his consciousness slipped away. He was breathing but was no longer able to respond. I decided to sing to him. I had said everything; now all I wanted to do was sing. And I think he heard me. I think he did ...

Following his death, I have been overwhelmed with a different sense of his presence. It feels spiritual and otherworldly yet totally palpable. I feel his guidance in a quiet voice that makes me smile involuntarily every time I think of him.

Losing one's father creates an absence of a protective and guiding force. It's left a big void, which has led to the thought, *This is a calling to rely on God more.* I want to rely on faith more ... to dig up every bit of trust I can conjure up in life, because the human father is gone. I am actually grateful for this challenge—to amp up my faith, my trust, and my belief in something bigger than myself. I want to amp up my connection with God, to listen, and to believe that life is good and that life has my back. Love is the greatest force; we are all connected, and there is a point. The point is to be at peace with ourselves, yes, and to find faith that our desires and cravings matter and come from beyond us to teach us who we really are. My dad's love for me in life set the tone to help me move forward even in his absence. Love, as a guiding principle, really does the trick.